7 Steps to Profit From Purchasing Multifamily Properties

The ultimate Guide to Wealth Purchasing Multi-family Dwellings

Darkblue Wells

Table of Contents

Introduction	1
Understanding the Multifamily Market	5
Current Market Trends and Opportunities	6
Key Factors Influencing Property Values	10
Summary and Reflections	14
Identifying a Profitable Property	16
Utilizing Property Search Tools and Conducting Preliminary Market Research	17
Evaluating Neighborhood and Demographic Data	21
Final Insights	24
Comprehensive Property Analysis	26
Analyzing financial statements and rent rolls	27
Assessing property condition and required repairs	30
Final Thoughts	34
Financing Your Multifamily Purchase	35
Comparing Loan Types and Terms	36
Leveraging Private Financing and Syndications	39
Final Thoughts	43
Effective Negotiation Tactics	45
Preparing for negotiations with sellers	46
Utilizing contingencies to your advantage	48
Closing Remarks	52
Property Management Essentials	54
Hiring and Managing Property Management Teams	55

Maintaining Tenant Relations and Ensuring Proper Upkeep	59
Core Message	61
Maximizing Profit and Scaling Your Portfolio	63
Refinancing and Reinvesting Profits	64
Implementing Value-Add Strategies and Planning for Long-Term Growth	67
Final Insights	71
Conclusion	73

Chapter 1
Introduction

Did you know that multifamily properties have consistently outperformed single-family homes, with a staggering appreciation of 30% in the last decade alone? This striking statistic underscores the tremendous growth potential within the multifamily real estate market. It's not just numbers on a page; it's a glimpse into how a strategic investment in this sector can become a powerful engine for wealth creation and financial stability.

Real estate is often touted as one of the most reliable avenues for building wealth, but among its many branches, multifamily investing stands out for several compelling reasons. For starters, investing in multifamily properties means you're not putting all your eggs in one basket. A duplex, triplex, or apartment complex reduces your risk by spreading it across multiple units. If one tenant moves out, the others continue to generate rental income, providing a steady and more predictable cash flow than single-family rentals can offer.

Moreover, multifamily properties allow you to scale your investment portfolio more efficiently. Consider this: managing ten single-family homes scattered across different locations requires ten separate transactions and likely ten times the effort in terms of maintenance and management. On the other hand, a 10-unit apartment building consolidates those efforts into one location, making it easier to manage and significantly reducing operational headaches. It's this ability to scale that makes multifamily investing a financially attractive option.

Throughout this guide, you will discover a systematic seven-step approach designed to take you from a novice investor to a savvy multifamily property owner. Each step has been carefully crafted to demystify the process and provide you with actionable insights. We'll begin with foundational concepts such as understanding market dynamics and identifying lucrative opportunities, then move on to more sophisticated topics like financing strategies, effective property management, and ultimately, scaling your portfolio for long-term success. These steps are not random but a cohesive framework distilled from years of experience and proven success stories.

So, what makes these strategies so adaptable and effective? The beauty of multifamily investing lies in its versatility. Whether you're starting with little to no knowledge of real estate or you're an experienced investor looking to diversify your holdings, the principles outlined in this book are designed to meet you where you are. You'll find practical tips and real-world examples that illustrate how investors at various stages have successfully navigated the market. Even if you're a complete beginner, the strategies shared in this book have empowered countless investors to dive into the multifamily market successfully. You don't need a wealth of experience to get started; you just need the right guidance and a willingness to learn.

However, technical knowledge alone won't guarantee your success in the multifamily arena. Equally important is adopting the right mindset. Imagine shifting from a scarcity mindset to one of abundance, where every property you analyze brings you closer to financial freedom and wealth-building opportunities. This mental shift transforms obstacles into challenges and setbacks into learning experiences. Being proactive, staying curious, and maintaining an open mind are essential traits that will serve you well on this journey. Remember, success in real estate is as much about perseverance and mindset as it is about market analysis and deal structuring.

As we embark on this journey together, I encourage you to actively engage with the content. Take notes, ask questions, and visualize how each concept applies to your unique situation. By doing so, you'll not only deepen your understanding but also build the confidence needed to make informed decisions.

In conclusion, multifamily real estate investing offers an unparalleled opportunity to grow your wealth and achieve financial independence. With its inherent advantages—such as risk diversification, scalable opportunities, and consistent income streams—multifamily investing is a cornerstone strategy for any serious real estate investor. This book aims to equip you with the knowledge, tools, and mindset necessary to succeed in this dynamic market.

So, let's get started on turning your multifamily investment dreams into reality. Whether you aspire to own a small duplex or an expansive apartment complex, the journey begins now. Together, we'll explore the ins and outs of this exciting venture, breaking down complex topics into digestible, actionable steps. By the end of this guide, you'll not only understand the intricacies of multifamily investing but also feel empowered to make your first —or next—investment with confidence. Welcome to the world of multifamily real estate. Your path to financial freedom and wealth-building opportunities starts here.

Chapter 2
Understanding the Multifamily Market

Understanding the multifamily market landscape involves recognizing how different factors influence investment opportunities and property values. As emerging rental trends reshape tenant preferences, investors need to stay attuned to what renters value most, such as modern amenities and prime locations. These preferences are not just about comfort but directly impact occupancy rates and rental income potential. By aligning property offerings with current renter demands, investors can enhance their appeal and achieve better returns on their investments.

This chapter delves into various aspects that shape the multifamily real estate market. You'll explore the impact of economic factors like interest rates and employment levels on property values and rental demand. The discussion also covers technological advancements that make properties more attractive and efficient to manage. Additionally, the influence of government policies and incentives will be examined, showcasing how investors can leverage these to their advantage. Understanding these components will not only help you navigate the market more effectively but also position you for long-term success in the multifamily real estate sector.

Current Market Trends and Opportunities

Emerging Rental Trends

The multifamily real estate market is experiencing significant changes driven by emerging rental trends. Understanding these trends can provide a strategic advantage to investors. One major shift involves renters' increasing preference for amenities and prime locations. Modern amenities such as fitness centers, coworking spaces, pet-friendly facilities, and high-speed internet are no longer just added bonuses; they are becoming essential features that attract tenants. Properties located near public transportation, good schools, and vibrant community centers also tend to be more appealing.

Recognizing these preferences enables investors to choose properties with greater renter appeal. By tailoring property offerings to align with these trends, investors can increase occupancy rates and thus, improve their returns. For instance, adding or upgrading amenities based on current tenant demands can transform an ordinary building into a highly sought-after rental property.

Additionally, understanding these shifts in renter preferences can significantly inform investment timing and location choices. Investors who are aware of where the demand is heading can strategically acquire properties in high-growth areas before prices soar. This proactive approach not only maximizes investment potential but also positions investors ahead of market competitors.

Impact of Economic Factors

Economic factors play a crucial role in the dynamics of the multifamily market. Variables such as interest rates, employment rates, and overall economic health directly impact both property values and rental demand. Low-interest rates generally make financing more accessible and affordable for investors, encouraging more purchases in the sector. Conversely, high-interest rates can dampen property acquisitions due to increased borrowing costs.

Employment rates also have a direct correlation with rental demand. High employment levels typically lead to increased demand for rental properties as more individuals have stable incomes to afford rent. On the other hand, rising unemployment can result in higher vacancy rates as more people struggle financially and cannot sustain rental payments.

Understanding these economic indicators gives investors a competitive edge in property selection. For example, being aware of upcoming interest rate hikes can prompt investors to secure fixed-rate mortgages to hedge against future cost increases. This understanding also aids in forecasting potential downturns or uptrends in the market, allowing investors to make informed decisions about when to buy or sell properties.

Investors must be keenly aware of cyclical behaviors in the real estate market to optimize investment timing. During economic booms, property values and rental incomes usually rise, making it an opportune time to invest. However, during economic downturns, having a thorough understanding of market cycles can help investors avoid overpaying for properties or getting caught in declining markets.

Technological Advancements

Technology continues to shape the multifamily real estate market landscape, creating new opportunities for investors. Smart building features, such as energy-efficient systems, security enhancements, and smart home devices, are becoming increasingly popular among renters. These innovations not only enhance property desirability but also offer long-term cost savings through improved energy efficiency and reduced maintenance requirements.

Investors should prioritize tech-savvy properties to attract modern tenants who value these conveniences. Implementing smart technology in properties can set them apart from traditional buildings, offering a unique selling point.

Furthermore, staying updated on technology-driven demand can reveal novel investment opportunities, such as properties equipped with comprehensive IoT systems or those designed to support co-living arrangements.

Leveraging technology also improves property management efficiency, ultimately maximizing profit margins. Property management tools, like digital lease signing, online rent payment systems, and automated maintenance requests, streamline operations and reduce administrative burdens. This efficiency allows investors to focus on expanding their portfolios and enhancing tenant satisfaction.

Government Policies and Incentives

Government policies and incentives play a significant role in shaping the multifamily real estate market. Regulations at the federal, state, and local levels can impact everything from property development to rental income. For instance, knowledge of grant programs or tax incentives can provide substantial financial advantages to investors. Taking advantage of these programs can reduce overall investment costs and improve profitability.

Understanding local zoning laws is another vital aspect for investors. Zoning regulations dictate what can be built and where, potentially revealing hidden opportunities for development or acquisition. For example, areas rezoned for higher density residential use could present lucrative prospects for constructing multifamily buildings. Navigating these legal frameworks effectively requires a thorough understanding of the specific regulations in the region of interest.

Awareness of government policies can guide strategic investments in regions poised for growth. Regions with favorable housing policies, infrastructure development plans, or economic incentives are likely to see increased demand for rental properties. Thus, keeping abreast of policy changes can enable investors to identify and capitalize on emerging markets, positioning themselves for long-term success.

Key Factors Influencing Property Values

Understanding the critical elements that determine the value of multifamily properties is essential for making smarter investment choices. By diving into key aspects such as location dynamics, property conditions and features, market demand and supply, and rental income potential, investors can better navigate the multifamily real estate landscape to maximize their returns.

First and foremost, location dynamics play a pivotal role in determining the desirability and value of multifamily properties. The age-old adage "location,

location, location" holds true for good reason. Investors should prioritize high-demand areas to maximize rental income potential. High-demand locations often offer access to amenities, public transport, good schools, and employment opportunities, all of which make properties more attractive to potential renters.

In addition to established high-demand areas, information on upcoming neighborhoods can help identify potential hidden gems. These are areas that may not yet be fully developed but show promise due to factors like planned infrastructure projects or economic development initiatives. Investing in such emerging markets can lead to significant appreciation as the neighborhood grows and matures.

Understanding local demographics is equally important, as it enables targeted marketing strategies that enhance occupancy rates. For example, a property located near a university may have a higher occupancy rate if marketed towards students, while a property in a family-friendly suburb might do better with amenities catering to young families. Tailoring marketing efforts to the specific demographics of an area helps ensure a steady stream of tenants and reduces vacancy rates.

Next, investigating how the age, style, and amenities of a property contribute to its value is crucial. Assessing value through property features facilitates informed buying decisions. Properties with modern designs, energy-efficient appliances, and updated amenities tend to attract higher-quality tenants willing to pay premium rents.

Understanding the impact of renovations on property value is another essential aspect. Renovations can significantly increase a property's market value and rental income potential. However, it's vital to prioritize renovations that offer the best return on investment. For example, updating kitchens and bathrooms often yields higher returns compared to less impactful upgrades like painting walls or replacing carpets.

Differentiating high-value features from standard ones can also help tailor potential upgrades to maximize returns. Features like in-unit laundry, secure parking, and advanced security systems can set a property apart from competitors, making it more attractive to renters and justifying higher rent prices. Understanding which amenities are most valued by renters in a particular area can guide investment priorities and boost overall profitability.

Fluctuations in market demand and supply directly affect pricing. Recognizing signs of an oversupplied market is vital to avoid purchasing properties whose values are likely to decline. Signs of oversupply include a high number of vacant units in the area and an abundance of new constructions. When the supply outstrips demand, rental prices tend to stagnate or decrease, negatively impacting profitability.

Conversely, understanding local rental supply can directly influence acquisition strategies. Areas with limited rental supply and high demand often command higher rents and offer better returns on investment. Strategic purchasing during periods of high demand can yield healthier returns, as competition among renters drives up rental prices. For example, securing a property in an undersupplied market before a population boom can position investors to reap substantial benefits.

Projected rental income shapes property valuation significantly. Knowing fair market rents in target areas provides negotiation ammunition when acquiring properties. Accurate knowledge of current market rents ensures that investors do not overpay for properties and helps in setting competitive yet profitable rental rates.

Analyzing comparable rental units allows investors to assess the true income potential of a property. This involves comparing similar properties in terms of size, location, and amenities to understand what rents they fetch. Such comparisons give a realistic picture of the income one can expect from a particular investment.

Understanding vacancy trends is also critical in mitigating risks associated with rental income fluctuations. High vacancy rates indicate potential issues, such as overpricing or poor property management. Conversely, low vacancy rates suggest strong demand and stable rental income. Investors should strive to maintain low vacancy rates through effective marketing and competitive pricing strategies.

For instance, offering flexible lease terms or small incentives such as a month's free rent can attract more tenants and keep vacancy rates low. Additionally, understanding seasonal patterns in rental demand can help investors plan for vacancies better. Some areas experience higher demand during certain times of the year, such as college towns during the start of academic terms.

To encapsulate, the location of a property sets the stage for its income potential and investment viability. High-demand areas and emerging neighborhoods offer substantial growth opportunities. Property condition and features significantly influence value, with modern amenities and thoughtful renovations boosting attractiveness and returns.

Summary and Reflections

Throughout this chapter, we've delved into the multifamily real estate market, examining current rental trends, economic factors, technological advancements, and government policies that shape investment potential. We discussed how modern amenities and prime locations attract renters, increasing occupancy rates and returns. We also highlighted the importance of understanding economic indicators like interest rates and employment levels, which directly impact property values and rental demand.

The chapter further explored how integrating smart technology can set properties apart and improve management efficiency. We underscored the significance of being knowledgeable about government incentives and local zoning laws to uncover hidden opportunities. By leveraging these insights, investors can strategically choose properties, optimize their portfolios, and stay ahead of market competitors. The goal is to equip you with the knowledge needed to make well-informed decisions in the dynamic multifamily real estate landscape.

Chapter 3
Identifying a Profitable Property

Identifying profitable investment opportunities is essential for anyone looking to succeed in the real estate market, especially when it comes to multifamily properties. In today's digital world, there are numerous tools and resources available that can make this process much easier and more efficient. By leveraging these modern aids, investors can save time and money while making well-informed decisions about which properties have the greatest potential for high returns. Whether you're a seasoned investor or just starting out, understanding how to utilize these tools can provide a solid foundation for your investment journey.

This chapter will guide you through various property search tools and methods for conducting preliminary market research, helping you identify lucrative multifamily properties. You'll learn about online listing platforms like Zillow and LoopNet, which offer extensive databases of properties and advanced search features. Additionally, the chapter covers specialized real estate investment software that analyzes property performance and market trends. We'll also delve into the importance of evaluating economic indicators such as employment rates and population growth, as well as the role of market analysis reports in identifying emerging neighborhoods. By mastering these skills, you'll be equipped to pinpoint investment opportunities with confidence and ensure long-term success in the real estate market.

Utilizing Property Search Tools and Conducting Preliminary Market Research

In today's digital age, investors have access to a plethora of tools and resources that can significantly simplify the process of locating and evaluating profitable multifamily properties. This section provides an insightful look into these digital aids, equipping you with the knowledge to make well-informed investment decisions.

One of the most valuable resources for real estate investors is online listing platforms. Websites such as Zillow, Realtor.com, and LoopNet offer extensive listings of multifamily properties. These platforms allow investors to perform targeted searches based on specific criteria such as location, price range, property size, and more. For instance, if you're interested in properties within a certain budget, you can filter your search to only include listings that match your financial parameters. Beyond just listings, many of these sites include detailed property descriptions, high-quality photographs, and even virtual tours. This means you can get a fairly comprehensive initial evaluation without needing to set foot on the property, saving time and money.

Moreover, many of these online platforms offer additional features like setting alerts for new listings that match your criteria. This ensures that you never miss out on potential opportunities. Imagine having a system that notifies you every time a multifamily property in a high-demand area becomes available—it's like having a dedicated assistant who's always on the lookout for you.

In addition to listing platforms, specialized real estate investment software can be a game-changer for investors. Tools like RealData, Stessa, and DealCheck are designed specifically to assist real estate investors in analyzing property performance. These programs allow you to input various metrics such as purchase price, rental income, expenses, and financing details. The software then calculates key investment indicators like cash flow, cap rate, and return on investment (ROI). This detailed analysis helps you understand the potential profitability of a property before making a purchase decision.

Many of these tools also offer market analysis features that provide insights into local real estate trends. For example, they may show historical data on property values, rent prices, and occupancy rates. Having access to this information empowers investors to make informed decisions based on reliable data, rather than guesswork. Moreover, the ability to streamline the investment process through automated calculations and data interpretation instills confidence in your evaluations and decision-making.

Another critical aspect of evaluating potential investments is understanding economic indicators. Key factors such as employment rates and population growth play a crucial role in assessing the long-term viability of rental income. High employment rates often correlate with a stable economy, meaning tenants are more likely to afford rent consistently. Similarly, population growth indicates a demand for housing, which can lead to higher occupancy rates and potentially increased rental prices. Investors should keep a close eye on these indicators when evaluating different markets to ensure the sustainability of their investments.

Market analysis reports are another essential tool for investors. Reports from sources such as CoStar, Yardi Matrix, and REIS offer comprehensive insights into market trends, demand, and rental prices. These reports often highlight emerging neighborhoods that are experiencing growth and could provide lucrative investment opportunities. By comparing these reports across different markets, investors can identify areas with strong potential for appreciation and better returns. For example, a market analysis report might reveal that a particular neighborhood is undergoing significant development, attracting businesses and new residents. Investing in such an area early on could result in substantial gains as the neighborhood continues to grow.

A practical application of these tools and methods can be illustrated through a hypothetical scenario. Suppose you are searching for a multifamily property in a mid-sized city. You start by using an online listing platform to narrow down properties that meet your criteria. After identifying a few potential options, you use a real estate investment software to analyze the financial performance of each property. The software reveals that one property has a higher projected cash flow and ROI compared to the others. Next, you review market analysis reports for the city and discover that the neighborhood where this property is located is poised for growth due to upcoming infrastructure projects and an influx of tech companies. Lastly, you check economic indicators and find that the city has low unemployment rates and steady population growth. Based on this thorough analysis, you decide to invest in the property with confidence, knowing it aligns well with your long-term goals.

Evaluating Neighborhood and Demographic Data

Assessing neighborhood characteristics and demographic data is crucial in pinpointing investment opportunities in multifamily properties. These factors ensure that investments align with tenant demands and provide optimal returns. By evaluating various elements such as crime rates, school quality, public transportation, demographic trends, rent prices, and proximity to amenities, investors can make informed decisions and maximize their return on investment.

Crime rates are a primary concern for potential tenants. A neighborhood with high crime rates will likely deter renters, leading to higher vacancy rates and decreased property appeal. Therefore, investors should investigate local police reports or use online tools like crime maps to gauge the safety of an area. Safe neighborhoods tend to attract more families and professionals, who often prefer longer leases, thereby ensuring a steady income stream for the investor.

School quality is another critical factor. Families with children prioritize good schools when choosing where to live. Investing in areas with reputable schools can lead to higher demand for rental properties, driving up rental prices and overall property value. Investors should research school district ratings and performance metrics to understand better how a nearby school might influence their property's desirability. Resources such as GreatSchools.org offer valuable insights into school quality and are easily accessible.

Accessibility to public transportation greatly influences neighborhood desirability. Many tenants prefer locations that allow easy commutes to work, shopping centers, and recreational activities. Properties located near bus stops, subway stations, or major highways often command higher rents. To capitalize on this, investors can leverage online transit maps and local government resources to evaluate the accessibility of public transportation in potential investment areas.

Understanding demographic trends is vital for aligning property features and marketing strategies with tenant preferences. Demographic data, such as population growth, income levels, and age distributions, inform investors about the type of tenants they can expect to attract. For instance, a neighborhood witnessing significant population growth suggests a rising demand for housing. Conversely, stagnant or declining populations might indicate challenges in maintaining occupancy rates. Tools like the U.S. Census Bureau and local government websites provide valuable demographic information.

Income levels within a neighborhood help investors determine appropriate rent pricing and property upgrades. Higher-income areas can support higher rental prices and possibly luxury amenities, while lower-income areas might require more affordability-focused strategies. Understanding the financial capabilities of potential renters ensures that investors set competitive yet profitable rental rates.

Age distribution is another demographic component that impacts investment strategies. Younger populations might prefer modern, smaller apartments with easy access to nightlife and social venues, whereas older populations may seek larger, quieter homes with proximity to healthcare services. By tailoring property attributes to the dominant age group in an area, investors enhance tenant satisfaction and retention.

Comparing average local rent prices assists investors in setting competitive rental rates and projecting cash flow accurately. Investors can analyze local rent prices through resources like Zillow or Rentometer. Such comparisons reveal whether the proposed rental prices are in line with market expectations, allowing investors to optimize their pricing strategies to attract tenants while ensuring profitability. Accurate rent projections are key to understanding the property's revenue potential and planning for expenses like maintenance and renovations.

Proximity to amenities like shopping centers, parks, and healthcare services significantly enhances a property's appeal. Tenants appreciate easy access to daily necessities and leisure activities, making properties near these amenities more attractive. For example, a family might prioritize living near a good park for recreational purposes, while young professionals may prefer proximity to shopping and dining options. Healthcare facilities are particularly important for areas with aging populations, offering peace of mind and convenience.

When analyzing amenities, investors should consider not only their presence but also the quality and variety offered. A neighborhood with diverse dining options, boutique shops, and well-maintained parks is likely to be more desirable than one with limited, lower-quality amenities. Tools like Google Maps and local business directories can offer insights into the types and quality of amenities available.

Final Insights

This chapter has provided a comprehensive guide on how to identify profitable multifamily properties using a range of digital tools and resources. By leveraging online listing platforms, specialized real estate investment software, and market analysis reports, you can streamline your search process and make data-driven decisions. These tools help you evaluate property performance, understand local real estate trends, and stay informed about new opportunities that fit your investment criteria.

Additionally, we've discussed the importance of analyzing neighborhood characteristics and demographic data to ensure your investments align with tenant demands. Understanding factors such as crime rates, school quality, public transportation, and demographic trends can significantly impact property desirability and rental income stability. By incorporating these insights into your investment strategy, you're better equipped to make informed decisions that promise high returns and long-term success in the multifamily property market.

Chapter 4
Comprehensive Property Analysis

Performing comprehensive property analysis is key to making smart multifamily real estate investments. This involves looking at the financial health of the property and understanding the potential for income and expenses. By breaking down detailed financial statements, investors can get a clear picture of whether a property is truly profitable. Decoding income and balance sheets helps to identify any red flags and areas where spending might be cut or income might be increased. All these financial indicators give investors an edge in forecasting future performance and making well-informed decisions.

In this chapter, you'll learn how to evaluate financial documents like income statements and balance sheets to gauge a property's profitability. You'll also discover the importance of rent rolls in understanding tenant dynamics and potential income growth. The chapter delves into ratio analyses for deeper financial insights and teaches you how to interpret historical data to predict future trends. Additionally, it covers the essential steps in assessing the physical condition of properties, estimating repair costs, and prioritizing upgrades that add value. By mastering these skills, you'll be better equipped to make informed investment decisions that maximize returns.

Analyzing financial statements and rent rolls

Evaluating the financial viability of multifamily properties is essential for making informed real estate investment decisions. In order to assess this, it's important to understand the key components of income statements and balance sheets. These documents provide a snapshot of the property's financial health and help in determining its profitability.

An income statement, often referred to as a profit and loss statement, details the revenue generated by the property and subtracts expenses to calculate net operating income (NOI). NOI is a critical measure because it reflects the profitability of the property before taking into account financing costs and taxes. To derive accurate insights, an investor should scrutinize each component on the income statement. Revenue sources typically include rental income, parking fees, and any other additional services provided to tenants. On the expense side, look for items such as property management fees, maintenance costs, insurance, and utilities. By understanding these elements, you can gauge operational efficiency and identify areas where costs may be reduced to boost profitability.

Next, take a close look at the balance sheet, which provides a broader overview of the property's assets, liabilities, and equity at a specific point in time. Key assets include the property itself, any improvements made, and accounts receivable from tenants. Liabilities could range from mortgage loans to unpaid bills for goods and services. The balance between these figures informs you about the financial stability of the property. When assessing a balance sheet, make sure to consider depreciation, which can offer tax benefits but does not impact cash flow directly.

Decoding rent rolls is another vital part of property analysis. A rent roll lists all tenant information, including rent amounts, lease terms, and occupancy status. Comparing market rent with current occupied rent allows investors to identify potential opportunities for increasing income. If rents are below market value, there may be room to increase them once leases expire. However, it's also essential to consider tenant turnover rates, as high turnover might result in increased vacancy periods and greater leasing costs. Analyzing rent rolls helps in forecasting income stability and identifying units that could benefit from upgrades or repositioning in the market.

Performing ratio analyses provides deeper financial insights into a multifamily property. One crucial ratio is the capitalization rate (cap rate), calculated by dividing the NOI by the purchase price of the property. This ratio indicates the expected rate of return on investment. A higher cap rate generally signifies a higher return but might also indicate higher risk. Conversely, a lower cap rate might suggest a more stable, albeit less lucrative, investment.

Another important metric is the cash-on-cash return, which measures the annual return made on the actual cash invested, excluding any mortgage. Calculating this involves dividing the annual pre-tax cash flow by the total cash invested. This figure gives insight into the immediate profitability and liquidity of the investment and helps compare different investment opportunities on an apples-to-apples basis.

Additionally, examining operating expense ratios can reveal how efficiently a property is being managed. This ratio is obtained by dividing total operating expenses by gross operating income. A high operating expense ratio may indicate that the property is incurring excessive costs, whereas a low ratio suggests efficient management and better profitability. It's crucial to compare these ratios with industry standards to determine whether a property's expenses are aligned with typical operational practices.

Interpreting historical data is another step in analyzing the financial viability of a multifamily property. Historical performance data provides context, allowing investors to discern trends and project future property performance. Review past income statements and balance sheets to understand how revenue and expenses have evolved over time. Look for patterns in occupancy rates, rent increases, and maintenance costs. This data can help you forecast future income and identify potential risks or opportunities.

Furthermore, analyzing year-over-year performance data can help you evaluate the stability of the property's income stream. Consistent income growth suggests a well-managed property with stable tenants, while erratic income patterns could signal underlying issues such as high tenant turnover or significant maintenance problems. By assessing these trends, investors can make more informed decisions about the property's long-term viability.

Assessing property condition and required repairs

Assessing the physical state of a property is essential for making informed investment decisions, particularly in the multifamily real estate market. This subpoint aims to arm readers with practical tools and techniques to evaluate a property's condition and identify necessary improvements that could influence profitability.

The first step in a comprehensive property analysis is conducting a thorough physical inspection. During this inspection, the focus should be on the structural integrity of the building and the condition of key systems such as plumbing, electrical, and HVAC. Begin by examining the foundation for any signs of cracks or shifts, which can indicate serious structural issues. Look at the roofing for wear and tear, as problems here can lead to water damage inside the property. Inspect the walls for any signs of bulging or cracking, which might suggest foundational problems.

It's also crucial to assess the condition of plumbing systems. Check for leaks, corrosion, and water pressure, as these can point to future costly repairs. Electrical systems should be inspected for outdated wiring, overloaded circuits, and compliance with current safety standards. Hiring a licensed electrician can provide a more detailed assessment of these aspects. In the case of HVAC systems, ensure they are functioning efficiently without any unusual noises or irregularities in performance. A professional inspection will help identify potential issues that might not be immediately visible.

After conducting the physical inspection, the next step is to develop skills in estimating repair costs accurately. This involves understanding the scope of the necessary repairs and obtaining quotes from reliable contractors. Start by breaking down the needed repairs into categories—minor, moderate, and major. Minor repairs may include small plumbing fixes or patching up drywall, while moderate repairs could involve replacing windows or repairing sections of the roof. Major repairs might entail significant structural work or complete system overhauls.

Building a network of trusted contractors is invaluable. These professionals can provide accurate estimates and timelines for the completion of various repairs. Always get multiple quotes to ensure you are receiving a fair price. Additionally, consider reserving funds for emergencies. Unexpected repairs can arise even after a thorough inspection. Setting aside a contingency fund helps mitigate the financial impact of unforeseen issues and ensures that the property remains in good condition.

Evaluating improvement opportunities is another critical aspect of property analysis. Leveraging repairs for increased value can significantly enhance the property's appeal and profitability. One of the key strategies is to identify value-add renovations. These are improvements that not only address existing issues but also increase the property's overall value. For instance, upgrading kitchens and bathrooms can make living spaces more desirable, leading to higher rental rates and improved tenant retention.

Environmentally friendly upgrades can also boost property value. Installing energy-efficient appliances, adding insulation, and incorporating solar panels can reduce utility costs, which is attractive to both tenants and prospective buyers. Green improvements can often qualify for tax incentives or rebates, further enhancing their financial viability. Consider how each potential upgrade fits within your overall investment strategy and budget.

When prioritizing repairs and renovations, it is important to align them with the property's goals. Start by differentiating between urgent repairs and cosmetic changes. Urgent repairs, such as fixing a leaky roof or addressing electrical hazards, should take precedence as they directly impact the safety and habitability of the property. Cosmetic improvements, while important, can often be scheduled over a longer period.

To effectively plan your budget, categorize repairs and renovations based on their urgency and potential return on investment. Use a scoring system if necessary, ranking each task by its importance and impact on the property's value. This method provides a clear roadmap for addressing immediate concerns while also planning for long-term improvements.

Applying these guidelines allows investors to make strategic decisions about where to allocate resources most efficiently. By understanding the nuances of property inspections, estimating repair costs accurately, evaluating value-add opportunities, and prioritizing tasks, you can enhance the overall quality and profitability of your real estate investments.

Final Thoughts

In this chapter, we delved into the critical elements of evaluating multifamily investments through financial analysis. By examining income statements and balance sheets, investors can gain a clear picture of a property's profitability and financial stability. Understanding the nuances of rent rolls and performing ratio analyses further aids in assessing operational efficiency and potential returns. These steps are essential for making informed investment decisions that could significantly impact overall profitability.

Additionally, we explored the importance of a thorough property condition assessment. Conducting detailed inspections, estimating repair costs accurately, and identifying value-add opportunities are crucial for maintaining and enhancing property value. Building a reliable network of contractors and prioritizing repairs and upgrades based on urgency and return on investment are key strategies. Following these guidelines helps investors allocate resources efficiently and ultimately boosts the quality and profitability of their real estate ventures.

Chapter 5
Financing Your Multifamily Purchase

Financing your multifamily purchase involves understanding various loan options and strategies tailored to different investment scenarios. Each financing option comes with its own set of terms, benefits, and potential drawbacks that can significantly impact your investment's profitability and sustainability. As you embark on this journey, it's essential to have a clear grasp of these nuances so you can make informed decisions that align with your financial goals.

In this chapter, we'll delve into several financing avenues available for multifamily purchases. We'll start with conventional loans, scrutinizing their requirements and suitability for different investor profiles. Then we'll move on to FHA loans, highlighting their accessibility for first-time investors and the specific conditions they entail. Commercial loans will be explored next, focusing on their alignment with larger property acquisitions. Lastly, we'll analyze Adjustable Rate Mortgages (ARMs), weighing their initial advantages against possible future risks. By the end of this chapter, you'll have a comprehensive understanding of the financing landscape, enabling you to choose the right funding source for your multifamily investment.

Comparing Loan Types and Terms

When it comes to financing your multifamily property purchase, understanding the different types of loans available is crucial. Each loan type has unique characteristics, making some more suitable than others, depending on your financial situation and investment goals.

First, let's dive into conventional loans. These are typically offered by banks and credit unions and are one of the most common types of financing for multifamily investments. Conventional loans usually require a lower down payment compared to other financing options, which can be particularly appealing if you're trying to preserve cash flow for additional investments or reserve funds. The terms of these loans are often straightforward and predictable, with fixed or adjustable interest rates available, depending on your preference. However, it's important to note that while the smaller down payment requirement is attractive, conventional loans often come with stricter credit score requirements and debt-to-income ratios. Therefore, potential investors need to ensure their financial health aligns with these conditions.

Next up are FHA loans, which are insured by the Federal Housing Administration. These loans are especially beneficial for first-time investors who may not have substantial capital upfront. FHA loans allow for significantly lower down payments—sometimes as low as 3.5%—and are known for their more lenient credit requirements. This makes them accessible to a broader range of investors. However, one caveat to keep in mind is that FHA loans do come with strict property standards and mortgage insurance premiums, which can affect the overall cost of borrowing. These factors should be weighed carefully to determine if an FHA loan is indeed the best fit for your investment strategy.

Commercial loans are another valuable tool in the multifamily investor's arsenal. Unlike conventional and FHA loans, commercial loans are designed specifically for larger properties, typically those with five units or more. Banks and other lending institutions base these loans on the property's projected income rather than the borrower's personal financial health. This can be advantageous if you are investing in a high-income property but may present challenges if the property's income isn't reliably consistent. Commercial loans often come with varying terms, including balloon payments and shorter amortization periods. These terms require careful attention to ensure they align with your financial planning and long-term investment strategy.

Then there are Adjustable Rate Mortgages, or ARMs. ARMs can offer lower initial fixed rates, which might seem attractive during the early years of the loan. For investors expecting to sell or refinance before the rate adjusts, this can result in significant savings. However, the risk comes when the fixed-rate period ends, leading to potential rate adjustments based on market conditions. These adjustments can increase your monthly payments, sometimes substantially. Understanding the cap limits on rate changes and thoroughly analyzing market trends can help mitigate some risks associated with ARMs, making them a viable option for experienced investors comfortable with variable financial scenarios.

Choosing the right loan for your multifamily investment isn't just about comparing interest rates or down payment requirements—it's about considering how each loan type fits into your overall investment strategy and long-term financial goals. A close examination of your financial situation, the specific characteristics of the property you intend to purchase, and your future investment plans will guide you in making the best choice.

For instance, if you're new to multifamily investing and looking to start small with lower upfront costs, an FHA loan might be the ideal starting point. On the contrary, if you're planning to acquire larger properties or expand your portfolio rapidly, commercial loans might provide the flexibility and terms suited to such ventures. Meanwhile, conventional loans offer stability and predictability, especially valuable for long-term holdings where stable cash flow is paramount.

Moreover, while ARMs can be tempting due to their lower initial rates, they require a more nuanced understanding and management of potential future financial impacts. If you opt for an ARM, it's essential to stay informed about market trends and have a solid contingency plan to handle possible rate increases without jeopardizing your investment.

Leveraging Private Financing and Syndications

Financing a multifamily property can feel like a daunting task, but with the right strategies, it becomes much more manageable. One alternative to traditional financing is using private money lenders. These lenders are individuals or companies willing to invest their own funds into real estate ventures. Unlike banks, private money lenders often provide quicker access to cash and have more flexible terms.

One of the major advantages of private money lenders is the speed and ease with which you can secure financing. Traditional lenders come with exhaustive requirements, from credit checks to income verifications, which can slow down the approval process. In contrast, private lenders are primarily concerned with the property's potential rather than your financial history. This makes private lending an attractive option for those who might not meet the stringent criteria set by banks but possess promising real estate opportunities.

When working with private money lenders, it's crucial to establish clear terms. This includes agreeing on interest rates, repayment schedules, and any additional fees. Transparency and mutual understanding help in building a trustworthy relationship, ensuring smooth transactions. Private money loans typically carry higher interest rates than conventional loans due to the increased risk taken by the lender. Nonetheless, the quick access to funds and fewer hoops to jump through make this option appealing.

Now let's turn to real estate syndication. Syndication allows multiple investors to pool their resources together to acquire larger multifamily properties. This strategy spreads risk across all participants while enabling them to access investment opportunities that might be out of reach individually.

A typical syndication involves a sponsor or lead investor who identifies a profitable property and organizes the deal. The sponsor may not always contribute a large amount of capital but will manage the investment and oversee its progress. Investors, sometimes referred to as limited partners, provide the bulk of the funding and share in the returns. This collaborative model means that each party contributes differently, often complementing each other's strengths and resources.

The benefits of syndication are numerous. By pooling resources, investors can diversify their portfolios without putting too much capital into one single property. This diversification minimizes individual risk and provides a safety net against market fluctuations. Additionally, investors gain access to professional management through the sponsor, which can enhance the property's performance and increase returns.

Crowdfunding has emerged as another innovative way to finance multifamily properties. This approach leverages online platforms to attract a broad audience of potential investors. Crowdfunding democratizes real estate investing by opening the doors to those who might not have large sums of money or extensive networks of contacts.

In crowdfunding, project leaders present their real estate plans on specialized websites, detailing projected returns, risks, and timelines. Interested parties can then contribute varying amounts to fund the property acquisition. This process is often accompanied by rigorous due diligence conducted by the platform itself, providing additional security to potential investors.

For the younger generation of tech-savvy investors, crowdfunding offers an easy entry point into the real estate market. It provides transparency and convenience, allowing participants to track their investments online and receive regular updates. However, just like any other investment, it's essential to conduct personal research and understand the specific platform's fees and structures before participating.

Joint ventures represent another effective way to finance multifamily properties. A joint venture (JV) occurs when two or more parties come together to undertake a specific business endeavor. In real estate, JVs enable investors to combine their resources and expertise to purchase, manage, and potentially sell multifamily properties.

Each partner in a JV typically brings something unique to the table. One partner might possess industry knowledge and experience, while another contributes significant capital or property management skills. This synergy allows the JV to operate more efficiently and maximize profits.

Setting up a joint venture involves drafting a comprehensive agreement outlining each partner's roles, contributions, and profit-sharing arrangements. This clarity helps prevent misunderstandings and ensures all parties are aligned towards the same goals. Furthermore, having multiple stakeholders means that decision-making processes can benefit from diverse perspectives, leading to well-rounded strategies and solutions.

By collaborating, JV partners can tackle larger and more lucrative projects than they could individually. They also spread the financial burden and risk, making it easier to withstand potential setbacks. It's crucial, however, to choose JV partners wisely. Trust, compatibility, and shared objectives are key elements for a successful partnership.

Final Thoughts

Understanding the various financing options for purchasing multifamily properties equips you with the knowledge to make informed investment decisions. We've covered conventional loans, which offer stability but come with stricter requirements, and FHA loans, ideal for first-time investors due to their lower down payment needs. Commercial loans cater to larger property investments based on projected income, while ARMs provide flexibility with initial low rates but require careful management of future rate changes. Choosing the right loan type depends on your financial health, property characteristics, and long-term goals.

Additionally, alternative financing methods like private money lenders, real estate syndication, crowdfunding, and joint ventures can offer more flexible terms and access to capital. Private money lenders focus on the property's potential rather than your financial history, while syndications allow multiple investors to pool resources for larger deals. Crowdfunding democratizes investment opportunities, and joint ventures combine different strengths to tackle bigger projects. By exploring these options, you can find the best strategy that aligns with your investment plans and helps you succeed in the multifamily property market.

Chapter 6
Effective Negotiation Tactics

Mastering effective negotiation tactics is essential for securing favorable purchase terms in real estate. Negotiating can be complex, but with the right strategies, you can significantly improve your chances of getting the best deal possible. This chapter will provide you with practical techniques to interact successfully with sellers, helping you understand their motivations and developing a tailored approach that appeals to their interests.

In this chapter, we'll cover various key areas to prepare you for successful negotiations. You'll learn the importance of understanding the seller's reasons for selling, establishing your financial limits before engaging in discussions, and creating clear lists of priorities and concessions. Additionally, we will explore how practicing negotiation techniques through role-playing can enhance your skills. By the end of this chapter, you'll be equipped with the knowledge needed to confidently navigate negotiations and secure terms that benefit both you and the seller.

Preparing for negotiations with sellers

To effectively negotiate in real estate, you need to be well-prepared. This preparation can significantly increase your chances of securing favorable terms. Let's dive into some key strategies that will help you achieve this.

First and foremost, understanding the seller's motivation is crucial. Why is the seller putting their property up for sale? Are they relocating for a job, downsizing due to lifestyle changes, or perhaps facing financial difficulties? Each scenario presents unique opportunities. For instance, a seller needing a quick sale may be more flexible on price, whereas someone selling for emotional reasons might value sincerity and empathy over monetary gains. By tailoring your approach based on what drives the seller, you'll be better equipped to craft offers that appeal to their interests and increase your chances of success.

Equally important is establishing your budget and limits beforehand. Knowing your financial boundaries protects you from making impulsive decisions driven by emotions mid-negotiation. It helps maintain discipline, ensuring you don't agree to terms that could strain your finances later on. Begin by evaluating your current financial situation and determining a maximum offer you can comfortably afford. Also, factor in potential costs such as repairs, renovations, and closing expenses. With these figures in hand, you can confidently participate in discussions without the fear of overextending yourself financially.

Next, creating a list of priorities and concessions is essential. Before engaging in negotiations, identify your non-negotiables — aspects that are must-haves for you. These might include the property's location, size, or condition. Simultaneously, consider areas where you are willing to compromise. Maybe you're flexible on the closing date or willing to cover minor repair costs. Having this clear distinction allows you to stay focused during talks and quickly adapt if new information arises. It also shows sellers that while you have firm requirements, you are open to finding mutually beneficial solutions.

Practicing negotiation techniques is another vital component. Role-playing scenarios with a friend or colleague can sharpen your skills. This practice helps develop a persuasive communication style and prepares you for different responses from the seller. During these mock sessions, try out various tactics like active listening, asking open-ended questions, and using silence strategically. For example, after making an offer, remaining silent can pressure the seller to fill the void, often resulting in them revealing helpful information. Through consistent practice, you'll become more adept at reading body language, controlling the pace of conversations, and handling counteroffers confidently.

A practical guideline to follow when practicing negotiation techniques is to set up realistic role-playing exercises. Choose a partner who can impersonate different types of sellers, each with unique motivations and objections. Conduct multiple rounds focusing on different aspects of the negotiation process. Review each session critically, noting areas of strength and those needing improvement. Over time, this iterative process will build your confidence and proficiency, equipping you to handle even the most challenging negotiations with poise.

Utilizing contingencies to your advantage

Leveraging contingencies effectively can significantly add value to your offers and help manage risks in your real estate transactions. By understanding the different types of contingencies and knowing how to communicate their benefits, you can create deals that are appealing to both buyers and sellers.

First, it's essential to understand what contingencies are and how they function in real estate negotiations. Contingencies are conditions included in a purchase agreement that must be met before the contract becomes binding. They serve as safety nets to protect the interests of both parties involved. Some common types of contingencies include inspection contingencies, financing contingencies, and appraisal contingencies.

Inspection contingencies allow the buyer to have the property professionally inspected before finalizing the purchase. This ensures that any major issues or hidden defects are identified and addressed, either through repairs or price adjustments. For example, if an inspection reveals significant problems like a faulty roof or outdated electrical systems, buyers can request repairs or negotiate a lower purchase price to cover the costs of fixing these issues.

Financing contingencies protect the buyer by making the purchase dependent on securing a mortgage. Suppose a buyer is unable to obtain financing within a specified period. In that case, this contingency will allow them to back out of the deal without losing their earnest money deposit. This is crucial because it reduces the financial risk for the buyer, ensuring they do not commit to a purchase they cannot afford.

Appraisal contingencies ensure that the property is valued at or above the offer price. If the home appraises for less than the agreed-upon amount, the buyer has the option to renegotiate the price or walk away from the deal. This protects the buyer from overpaying and helps align the property's market value with the purchase price.

Now, constructing effective contingencies requires a strategic approach. While protecting your interests is vital, you also want to present contingencies in a way that does not deter sellers. Start by clearly defining what each contingency entails and set realistic terms and deadlines. For instance, instead of requesting a long inspection period, opt for a shorter, more reasonable timeframe that shows you are serious about moving forward quickly. This demonstrates respect for the seller's time and indicates that you are a motivated buyer.

Additionally, when drafting financing contingencies, be specific about the loan terms you are seeking. This may include the type of loan, interest rate, and any other relevant details. Providing this clarity helps sellers understand your financial standing and assures them that you are prepared and qualified to purchase their property.

Moreover, it is important to strike a balance between protection and appeal. Overly stringent contingencies might make your offer less attractive compared to others. Aim to create contingencies that safeguard your interests without causing unnecessary delays or complications. For example, rather than having multiple contingencies with vague terms, streamline them to focus only on the most critical aspects, presenting them in a well-organized manner.

Communicating the value of contingencies to sellers is another crucial step in the negotiation process. It's essential to frame contingencies not as hurdles but as mutual safeguards that benefit both parties. Explain how these conditions can build trust and facilitate a smoother transaction. For instance, an inspection contingency can reassure sellers that the buyer is genuinely interested in the property's condition, which can prevent potential disputes down the line. By presenting contingencies as tools that enhance transparency and accountability, you can foster a collaborative environment.

When discussing contingencies with sellers, emphasize the importance of trust and partnership. Highlight that these measures are designed to protect both sides and ensure that everyone is satisfied with the outcome. For example, letting sellers know that an appraisal contingency ensures the property's fair market value can help them see the logic behind it. This approach makes it easier for sellers to accept contingencies positively rather than viewing them as obstacles.

Handling contingency-related objections often arises during negotiations. Sellers may have concerns about the impact of contingencies on the timeline or potential additional costs. To address these objections effectively, be ready with thoughtful explanations and alternatives. For example, if a seller hesitates about a financing contingency due to past experiences with failed deals, explain how your solid pre-approval status and specific loan details mitigate this risk.

Flexibility and willingness to compromise can also go a long way in overcoming objections. If a seller prefers quicker closing, propose adjusting the inspection period while still retaining some level of protection. Offering solutions demonstrates your commitment to finding middle ground and maintaining a positive rapport. Remember, the goal is to create a win-win situation where both parties feel secure and valued.

Closing Remarks

Mastering negotiation techniques is a vital part of succeeding in real estate transactions. By understanding the seller's motivations, establishing your financial limits, and preparing a list of priorities and concessions, you can create compelling offers that cater to both parties' needs. Practicing negotiation through role-playing scenarios further refines your skills, making you more adept at managing conversations, reading body language, and handling counteroffers effectively.

Utilizing contingencies wisely also plays a crucial role in protecting your interests while keeping your offers attractive to sellers. Clearly defining and communicating the benefits of inspection, financing, and appraisal contingencies helps build trust and facilitates smoother transactions. Striking a balance between safeguarding your position and maintaining flexibility shows sellers that you are serious and well-prepared, creating win-win situations for all involved.

Chapter 7
Property Management Essentials

Effective management of multifamily properties relies on best practices that can enhance overall performance and profitability. This chapter delves into the essentials of property management, starting with how to hire and manage a capable property management team. A critical aspect of this process is evaluating the qualifications of potential managers, focusing on their certifications, experience, and essential soft skills. These elements collectively ensure that the chosen managers are well-equipped to handle tenant issues, maintain occupancy rates, and oversee emergency situations adeptly.

Following the selection of your property management team, the chapter explores setting clear expectations through detailed job descriptions and performance metrics. The importance of consistent communication and feedback is highlighted to foster an effective collaboration between you and your team. Additionally, adopting management software is discussed as a tool to streamline administrative tasks, improve financial reporting, and enhance overall efficiency. Lastly, the chapter covers maintaining strong tenant relations and implementing automated systems for rent collection and preventive maintenance, which are pivotal in sustaining a harmonious and efficient property management operation.

Hiring and Managing Property Management Teams

Evaluating Management Qualifications

In the realm of property management, selecting qualified managers is crucial. Qualified property managers bring a wealth of experience and a nuanced understanding of managing multifamily properties. When evaluating potential managers, look for individuals with certifications such as the Certified Property Manager (CPM) or Accredited Residential Manager (ARM). These titles indicate that the candidate has undergone rigorous training and adheres to high industry standards.

Experience is another vital consideration. A prospective manager should have a proven track record in handling properties similar to yours in size and scope. Ask for examples of how they've dealt with tenant issues, maintained occupancy rates, and handled emergency situations. This will give you a clear picture of their problem-solving abilities and resilience under pressure.

Moreover, soft skills are equally important. A competent property manager must excel in communication, be detail-oriented, and possess strong organizational skills. They need to manage not only the physical aspects of the property but also relationships with tenants and contractors. Effective negotiation skills can save money on vendor contracts and resolve tenant disputes amicably.

Setting Clear Expectations

Once you've selected your property management team, it's imperative to set clear expectations from the outset. This begins with detailed job descriptions outlining roles and responsibilities. Clearly delineate what tasks fall under their purview and which ones require your direct involvement.

Establishing performance metrics is essential in maintaining accountability. Metrics could include occupancy rates, tenant satisfaction scores, maintenance response times, and financial performance indicators like budget adherence. Regularly scheduled meetings can serve as checkpoints to review these metrics and address potential issues before they escalate.

Communication is key in setting these expectations. Use formal channels like email for official directives but also encourage informal check-ins to foster an open line of dialogue. This ensures that the management team feels supported and empowered to discuss challenges and successes openly.

Additionally, provide feedback – both positive and corrective. Commend the team for jobs well done to boost morale and motivation. Constructive criticism should be framed as opportunities for improvement rather than mere fault-finding. This balanced approach cultivates a culture of continuous improvement.

Building a Collaborative Relationship

Effective property management hinges on the strength of the relationship between you and your management team. It's critical to view this relationship as a partnership rather than a hierarchy. Collaboration fosters mutual respect and opens avenues for innovative solutions to common problems.

Engage with your team by regularly visiting the properties and participating in meetings. This hands-on approach demonstrates your commitment and provides valuable insights into day-to-day operations. Additionally, involve your team in strategic planning sessions. Their frontline experience offers perspectives that can fine-tune operational strategies and enhance property performance.

Encourage team-building activities that promote camaraderie and shared goals. Whether it's a simple team lunch or more structured team-building exercises, these activities can break down barriers and build trust. Remember, a harmonious team is more likely to perform efficiently and handle tenant concerns proactively.

It's also beneficial to establish a conflict resolution mechanism. Despite best efforts, disagreements may arise. Having a pre-structured process ensures that conflicts are addressed impartially and promptly, preventing them from hindering overall performance.

Implementing Management Software

Technology plays an increasingly significant role in enhancing property management efficiency. Implementing property management software can streamline several administrative tasks, allowing your team to focus on more strategic initiatives.

Software solutions can automate routine tasks such as rent collection, lease renewals, and maintenance scheduling. This automation reduces the risk of human error and ensures timely execution of essential functions. Moreover, most modern property management software includes features for financial reporting, providing real-time insights into property performance.

These tools also offer advanced communication capabilities. Tenants can report issues, make payments, and receive updates through a single platform, enhancing their overall experience. For the management team, it centralizes data and simplifies task tracking, enabling better coordination and follow-up.

When choosing software, consider the specific needs of your properties. Look for systems that offer customizable features, user-friendly interfaces, and robust customer support. Investing in training for your team to effectively utilize these tools is equally important. The initial time spent learning the system can result in long-term efficiencies and improved property management outcomes.

Maintaining Tenant Relations and Ensuring Proper Upkeep

Implementing automated rent collection is a game-changer in property management. Utilizing online platforms for rent collection offers several advantages that streamline the process and ensure timely payments. For instance, tenants can set up automatic payments, reducing the likelihood of late payments and overlooking due dates. This automation reduces administrative burden on property managers, who no longer need to chase down checks or manage cash deposits manually. By integrating an automated system, property managers also benefit from clear transaction records, making financial tracking and reporting more efficient and accurate.

Clear lease agreements are essential for maintaining a harmonious relationship with tenants and minimizing potential conflicts. Transparency in lease terms ensures that both parties understand their rights and obligations. A well-drafted lease should articulate the rent amount, due date, late fees, maintenance responsibilities, and other critical terms explicitly. Including clauses about property upkeep, tenant behavior expectations, and procedures for resolving disputes can preempt misunderstandings. When tenants know exactly what is expected, they are less likely to violate terms, which contributes to a smoother management experience. Furthermore, clearly defined leases provide legal protection for both landlords and tenants, helping to resolve any issues that might arise during the tenancy.

Establishing open communication channels between property managers and tenants fosters trust and encourages tenant retention. Tenants should feel comfortable voicing concerns without fearing repercussions. Creating multiple communication avenues—such as emails, phone calls, or a dedicated platform for maintenance requests—ensures tenants can reach out in the manner most convenient for them. Property managers should respond to inquiries and complaints promptly, demonstrating that tenant feedback is valued and considered. Regular check-ins or surveys can also proactively identify issues before they escalate. Encouraging this open dialogue helps build a sense of community and satisfaction among tenants, contributing to higher retention rates and positive word-of-mouth referrals.

A preventive maintenance schedule is crucial for avoiding significant repair issues and ensuring the property remains in good condition. Scheduling regular checks for essential systems like plumbing, electrical, and HVAC can help catch minor problems before they become major repairs. Routine inspections of common areas and individual units can highlight wear and tear that needs attention. Preventive maintenance not only protects the property's value but also enhances the living experience for tenants by reducing the likelihood of disruptive breakdowns. It demonstrates to tenants that their comfort and safety are a priority, thereby fostering goodwill and long-term loyalty.

Core Message

Effective management of multifamily properties hinges on selecting qualified managers, setting clear expectations, and fostering strong relationships. Qualified managers with certifications and experience are invaluable for handling tenant issues and maintaining occupancy rates. Clear job descriptions and performance metrics ensure accountability, while open communication and regular feedback help create a supportive work environment. Building a collaborative relationship further strengthens the management process, allowing for innovative solutions and mutual respect.

Additionally, leveraging technology through property management software streamlines administrative tasks like rent collection and maintenance scheduling. This not only reduces errors but also enhances overall efficiency. Transparent lease agreements and open communication channels with tenants foster trust and retention. Preventive maintenance schedules protect property value and tenant satisfaction by addressing minor issues before they escalate. By integrating these best practices, property owners can boost their property's performance and profitability through proactive management and tenant engagement.

Chapter 8
Maximizing Profit and Scaling Your Portfolio

Maximizing profit and scaling your multifamily investment portfolio involves strategic approaches to both financial management and property enhancement. This chapter delves into how you can unlock the potential of your investments through refinancing options, leveraging the concept of equity to reinvest and grow your assets. By understanding various refinancing methods, such as cash-out refinancing and rate-and-term refinancing, you'll learn to make informed decisions that align with your financial goals. Additionally, we'll explore essential metrics like return on investment (ROI) to ensure the benefits of refinancing outweigh the costs, providing you with a clear path to enhancing profitability.

Furthermore, this chapter discusses implementing value-add strategies and planning for long-term growth in your portfolio. You'll discover ways to identify and execute improvements that increase property value and appeal, while also integrating cost-saving enhancements like energy-efficient upgrades. Through thorough market research and diversification, you'll understand how to spread risk across different properties and locations, ensuring steady returns. Regularly adjusting your strategies based on performance metrics will help you stay ahead in the competitive real estate market, ultimately achieving sustained growth and profitability in your multifamily investments.

Refinancing and Reinvesting Profits

Refinancing can be a powerful tool for real estate investors looking to maximize profit and scale their portfolios. By understanding how to effectively utilize refinancing, you can unlock the equity in your properties and reinvest profits, thereby enhancing your investment capacity.

Firstly, let's delve into understanding equity. Equity accumulates over time through two main mechanisms: property appreciation and mortgage paydown. As the value of your property increases due to market conditions or improvements made, so does your equity. Concurrently, as you make mortgage payments, the amount you owe decreases, increasing your ownership stake in the property. This growing equity can serve as a financial resource that can be tapped into through refinancing.

There are various types of refinancing options available, each with its own implications. One common type is cash-out refinancing. This allows you to replace your existing mortgage with a new one that's higher than what you currently owe, taking the difference in cash. This option provides immediate funds that can be used for reinvestment or other purposes but often comes with higher interest rates and fees.

Another option is rate-and-term refinancing, which involves replacing your current mortgage with a new one that has better terms or a lower interest rate. This can reduce your monthly payments and increase your cash flow, but it doesn't provide immediate liquid funds like cash-out refinancing. It's essential to weigh the pros and cons of each type to determine which aligns best with your investment strategy.

Guideline: When considering refinancing options, it's crucial to evaluate your financial goals and current market conditions. Speak with a financial advisor or mortgage professional to explore the best option tailored to your situation.

Once you've unlocked equity through refinancing, strategic profit reinvestment becomes the next step. It's not enough to have capital; you need to deploy it wisely. Reinvesting profits into high-performing sectors of real estate can significantly enhance your portfolio's overall performance. For instance, consider investing in properties within emerging markets where growth potential is high, or in sectors like multifamily housing which tends to offer steady returns.

Additionally, diversification is key. Avoid putting all your funds into one type of property or location. Instead, spread your investment across various assets to mitigate risks and maximize returns. It's also beneficial to keep an eye on trends and innovations in the real estate market. Areas undergoing economic development or urban renewal projects can offer lucrative opportunities for reinvestment.

Guideline: Before reinvesting profits, conduct thorough market research to identify high-performing sectors and diversify your investments to balance risk and reward effectively.

To ensure that refinancing decisions are beneficial, calculating the return on investment (ROI) is critical. ROI metrics help evaluate whether the benefits of refinancing outweigh the costs involved. Start by calculating the net savings from reduced interest rates or monthly payments against the closing costs and fees associated with refinancing.

For example, if you opt for rate-and-term refinancing and reduce your interest rate by 1%, calculate the annual savings on interest. Compare this to the upfront costs of refinancing to determine how long it will take to break even—this is your payback period. A shorter payback period generally indicates a more favorable refinancing decision.

For cash-out refinancing, consider how effectively you can reinvest the cash obtained. If you use the funds to acquire another property that yields a high annual return, subtract the cost of refinancing from the projected income to gauge overall profitability.

Guideline: Utilize ROI metrics such as net savings, payback period, and projected income from reinvested funds to assess the effectiveness of your refinancing decisions. This ensures you're making informed choices that align with your financial objectives.

Implementing Value-Add Strategies and Planning for Long-Term Growth

Identifying Value-Add Opportunities

One of the first steps to maximizing profit in your multifamily investment portfolio is identifying value-add opportunities. These are areas where improvements can be made to boost the property's worth and appeal. Start by deeply analyzing existing properties. Look for underutilized spaces, outdated amenities, or maintenance issues. Conducting a thorough market analysis will help you understand what tenants value most in your area. For example, if other properties offer modern fitness centers or community rooms that attract higher rents, consider upgrading your property accordingly. Regularly conducting tenant surveys can also provide valuable insights into what improvements would make the biggest impact.

When assessing potential areas for improvement, look beyond cosmetic changes. Structural upgrades, like installing energy-efficient windows or updating plumbing systems, can reduce long-term operational costs and increase the property's value. Landscaping enhancements and curb appeal improvements can create a more inviting environment for current and prospective tenants. Remember, every dollar spent on adding value should ideally result in a greater return on investment, making it crucial to prioritize projects that offer the highest potential for increased revenue.

Cost-Saving Enhancements

Next, let's talk about cost-saving enhancements. Sustainable practices not only benefit the environment but also significantly cut down on operating costs. Begin by performing an energy audit to identify inefficiencies. Simple changes, like replacing incandescent bulbs with LED lighting or installing low-flow fixtures, can lead to substantial savings over time. Consider investing in programmable thermostats and energy-efficient appliances that can lower utility bills.

Waste reduction programs, such as recycling initiatives or composting, can also contribute to cost savings. Encourage tenants to participate by providing clear instructions and making recycling bins easily accessible. Another impactful improvement is enhancing insulation and sealing leaks. Proper insulation helps maintain indoor temperatures, reducing the need for excessive heating or cooling. Solar panel installations, although initially expensive, can provide long-term savings by generating renewable energy and potentially offering tax incentives.

Creating a Growth Strategy

To scale your multifamily property portfolio successfully, it's essential to create a well-defined growth strategy. Start by setting clear, achievable goals. Determine how many properties you aim to acquire within a specific timeframe and outline the resources needed to achieve this expansion. Streamlining your acquisition process will save time and ensure consistency. Develop a network of reliable real estate agents, mortgage brokers, and contractors to facilitate smooth transactions.

Diversification is key when expanding your portfolio. Avoid putting all your eggs in one basket by investing in properties across different locations and markets. This approach mitigates risks associated with economic downturns or local market fluctuations. Research emerging neighborhoods and trends that show potential for growth. Keep an eye on infrastructure developments, new business establishments, and population shifts, as these factors can influence property values.

Regularly reviewing your investment criteria is crucial. As you gain more experience, adjust your criteria based on past performance and market conditions. Be open to exploring different property types, such as student housing or senior living facilities, if they align with your overall objectives. A diversified portfolio not only spreads risk but also opens up new avenues for profit.

Reviewing and Adjusting Strategies

No strategy is foolproof, and the ability to adapt is paramount to long-term success. Continuously reviewing and adjusting your strategies ensures you stay ahead in the competitive real estate market. Performance metrics play a vital role in this process. Track key indicators such as occupancy rates, rental income, and maintenance expenses. Analyzing these metrics allows you to identify patterns and make informed decisions.

Communication with your property management team is essential. Schedule regular meetings to discuss ongoing projects, tenant feedback, and market trends. Utilize property management software to streamline operations and gather real-time data. This technology provides valuable insights into property performance, helping you pinpoint areas that need improvement.

Remain proactive in addressing issues that arise. If a particular property is consistently underperforming, investigate the root causes. It could be due to poor location, inadequate marketing, or tenant dissatisfaction. Implement targeted solutions to address these challenges, whether through strategic renovations, better marketing campaigns, or enhanced tenant services.

Remember, flexibility is key. The real estate market is constantly evolving, and sticking rigidly to a plan without considering external factors can be detrimental. Stay informed about economic trends, regulatory changes, and industry innovations. Embrace technology that simplifies property management and enhances tenant experiences. By regularly revisiting your strategies and making necessary adjustments, you'll position yourself for sustained growth and profitability.

Final Insights

This chapter has provided valuable insights into optimizing property performance and strategically expanding your multifamily investment portfolio. By leveraging refinancing, you can unlock the equity in your properties to enhance your investment capacity and reinvest profits wisely. We've discussed various refinancing options like cash-out and rate-and-term refinancing, each offering different benefits based on your financial goals. Furthermore, understanding the importance of recalculating ROI ensures that your refinancing decisions are informed and beneficial in the long run.

Equally important is identifying value-add opportunities and implementing cost-saving enhancements. Upgrading amenities, enhancing curb appeal, and adopting sustainable practices can significantly boost property values and reduce operating costs. Developing a clear growth strategy with defined goals, diversification, and flexibility will help you scale your portfolio effectively. Regularly reviewing and adjusting strategies based on performance metrics and market trends will keep you ahead in the competitive real estate market. By following these guidelines, you'll be well-equipped to increase profitability and support long-term growth in your multifamily investments.

Chapter 9
Conclusion

As we come to the end of our journey through the multifamily real estate landscape, let's take a moment to revisit the key insights we've uncovered together. These reflections will help solidify your understanding and prepare you for the steps ahead.

Throughout this book, we've explored the fundamentals of multifamily property investment, starting with the importance of grasping the multifamily market landscape. This foundational knowledge is crucial because, without it, you'd be investing with limited visibility. Understanding market trends, demographics, and economic indicators allows you to make informed decisions that can significantly impact the success of your investments.

We then delved into the financial criteria necessary for evaluating potential properties. Knowing how to analyze cash flow, return on investment, and other financial metrics ensures you're selecting properties that align with your investment goals. Remember, the numbers don't lie; they are your roadmap to profitable ventures.

Moreover, we discussed the significance of due diligence—examining every aspect of a property before making an offer. From physical inspections to tenant evaluations, thorough due diligence helps you avoid costly mistakes and protects your investment.

Next, we covered financing options and strategies, highlighting various ways to secure funding for your multifamily investments. Whether it's through traditional bank loans, private lenders, or creative financing methods, having access to capital is imperative for scaling your portfolio.

Managing your properties effectively was another critical area we addressed. Good property management not only maintains the value of your assets but also enhances tenant satisfaction and retention, leading to consistent rental income. We explored strategies for efficient property management, including finding reliable property managers and utilizing technology to streamline operations.

Now, equipped with these insights, it's time for action. Knowledge alone won't yield results unless it's applied. Start by identifying potential properties in your area that meet the financial criteria we've discussed. Use the tools and techniques you've learned to analyze these opportunities critically. Take that first step—it might be daunting, but every experienced investor started where you are now.

Imagine the long-term benefits of your efforts. Picture yourself five years from now, reflecting on a diversified multifamily portfolio that generates steady income and appreciates in value. This vision isn't just about financial gain; it's about creating a lasting legacy. Your investments can provide security and opportunities for you and your loved ones, building a foundation for future generations.

However, reaching this point requires more than initial action; it demands ongoing commitment. The real estate market is dynamic, influenced by economic shifts, policy changes, and evolving market conditions. To stay ahead, commit to continuous learning. Attend seminars, read up-to-date market analyses, and network with other investors. Staying informed keeps you adaptable and ready to capitalize on new opportunities.

Remember, investing in real estate is a marathon, not a sprint. Challenges will arise, but each obstacle is an opportunity to learn and grow. Every successful investor has faced setbacks, but perseverance and adaptability make all the difference. Stay focused on your long-term vision and remain flexible in your strategies.

In conclusion, the journey to success in multifamily real estate investment is paved with knowledge, action, and continuous learning. You've gained valuable insights into understanding market dynamics, evaluating financials, performing due diligence, securing financing, and managing properties. Now, it's up to you to apply these lessons and embark on your investment journey.

Take that leap—start analyzing properties, connect with industry professionals, and immerse yourself in the world of multifamily real estate. Visualize the future you want to create and work towards it relentlessly. This book has provided you with the foundation; now it's your turn to build upon it.

Embrace the challenges, celebrate the victories, and never stop learning. The multifamily market offers incredible opportunities for those willing to put in the effort. Your journey is just beginning, and with the right mindset and determination, the possibilities are endless. Here's to your success in multifamily property investment!